DAVID & GOLIATH

P9-ECK-944

Adapted by Tess Fries
Illustrated by Cheryl Mendenhall

DAVID & GOLIATH
Copyright © 2004 Spirit Press,
an imprint of Dalmatian Press, LLC.
All rights reserved

Art Directed by Shannon Osborne Thompson

SPIRIT PRESS and DALMATIAN PRESS are trademarks of
Dalmatian Press, LLC, Franklin, Tennessee 37067.
No part of this book may be reproduced or copied in any form
without the written permission of Dalmatian Press.

ISBN: 1-40370-971-8
11452-0804

Printed in the U.S.A.

04 05 06 07 LBM 10 9 8 7 6 5 4 3 2 1

Once there was a young shepherd boy named David. David was a happy boy, and he loved God very much. He wrote and sang many songs that told about God's power and His love for us.

One day David's father asked him to deliver some dried corn and ten loaves of bread to his three older brothers. They were fighting in the army of King Saul.

David left the next morning. When he got to the army camp on the mountain, he ran to see his brothers. How excited he was!

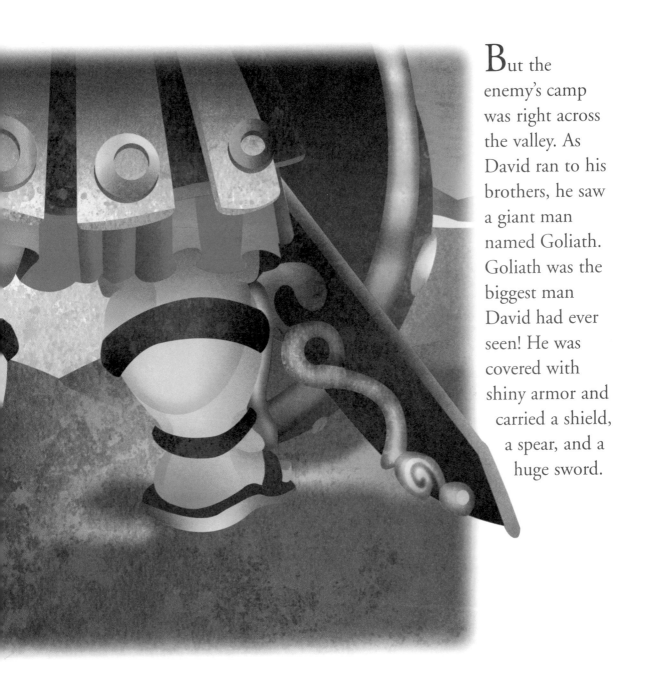

But the enemy's camp was right across the valley. As David ran to his brothers, he saw a giant man named Goliath. Goliath was the biggest man David had ever seen! He was covered with shiny armor and carried a shield, a spear, and a huge sword.

David's brothers told him that every morning and every night for forty days, Goliath had been shouting to them to send someone out to fight him. Goliath shouted, "If any of you can defeat me, your King's army will be the winner of the entire battle."

The King's soldiers were so afraid that they ran away each time they saw Goliath. But David was not afraid.

David went to the King and told him that he would fight Goliath! King Saul said, "You are much too small to fight this great giant." But David would not give up. He told the King that with God's help, he had defeated a fierce lion and a hungry bear who had stolen a lamb from his flock. David was sure that God would help him fight Goliath, too!

King Saul
believed that God
would help David
and insisted, "You
must take my
armor and sword
to fight a giant
such as Goliath."
David tried on
the armor and the
sword, but it was
too heavy for
him. So he took
only his staff and
sling and went
down to the river.

There at the river, David found five smooth stones and put them in his shepherd's bag.

Then David walked toward Goliath. Goliath laughed when he saw the small boy coming down the mountain toward him.

David said,
"I am not afraid!
God will help me."
Then he reached
into his bag and
pulled out one
smooth stone.

David put a stone in his sling and hurled it toward Goliath. It hit the giant directly on the forehead. The giant fell to the ground with a thud!

When the enemy soldiers saw that their mighty giant had fallen, they all ran away in fear.

With God's help, David had won the battle for King Saul.

When you think you are too young and too small to help someone else, remember how God helped David defeat the giant. Nothing is ever impossible for God, if only you let Him help you!

*"Reaching into his bag and taking out
a stone, he slung it and struck the
Philistine on the forehead."*
1 Samuel 17:49
(NIV)